(My) Life after Death

A Memoir of Milestones

Donna Kusman

Published in 2008 by YouWriteOn.com

Copyright © Text by Donna Kusman

First Edition

The author asserts the moral right under the Copyright, Designs and Patents Act 1988 to be identified as the author of this work.

All rights reserved.

No part of this publication may be reproduced, stored in a retrieval system, or transmitted, in any form or by any means, without the prior written consent of the author, nor be otherwise circulated in any form of binding or cover other than that in which it is published and without a similar condition being imposed on the subsequent purchaser.

Published by YouWriteOn.com

*For Jim Frederick, with much love,
for his care and feeding of all creatures great and small.*

(My) Life after Death

Milestones

The Mistress of Ceremonies

Precursor #1

Precursor #2

Not Quite 48

The Connection

Engraved in Stone

The Anniversary That Wasn't

An Uneventful 47

A Year without Santa Claus

Naked Hands

Welcome the New Year

Travelocity, Expedia, or Orbitz?

With This Ring

Kevin's Big Love

London Calling

Photo Op

Beyond the Bridge

Shreds of the Past

Saying Goodbye to Home

Saying Hello . . . Cheerio

Christmas in June

August in Paris

First

And in the End

The Mistress of Ceremonies

There were two things I'd settled on: First, I would read the e.e. cummings' poem "I Carry Your Heart with Me." Second, no make up.

The latter was an easier decision—the option of mascara-streaked tears with worn lipstick (or worse yet, only the liner remaining) versus tear-stained ruddy cheeks and pale lips kept the morning routine simple. Getting through the 14 lines of the poem worried me—I wanted to do it so badly, but the several hundred rehearsals the days before the wake left me in doubt. It did get easier with each run through, but I hadn't really made it through the entire poem without pause. I chose the poem because I'd sent it to Kevin on July 23—just 20 days before he died. I wanted him to know that I was thinking about him, that I loved him. I didn't know those 20 days before that I'd be reading it aloud to an audience of family and friends while his cremated remains stood four feet behind me in a silver matte urn with Kevin's name engraved into it.

I solicited a back-up; my dear friend Jill agreed to catch me if I faltered, to finish the lines for the people who came to the wake to hear the entire poem. Having her there just in case didn't really make me feel better—it was about me doing it all the way through—but there was some newly discovered strength in having her at hand, at having her say "I know you'll get through it" that put me in a better place. I did it. And three beats after the last word, I said aloud in amazement, "I did it"! I hadn't wanted to make the visitors chuckle at that, but I sensed some of them did. Where I did pause, just once, as told to me by my sister Debbie later, was at the words "a tree called life" . . . a bit out of synch for honoring the love of the dead. My voice softened, she said, so that perhaps the people in the back of the room had to strain to hear the rest—the remaining three verses. It didn't matter; I did it.

Several of Kevin's friends got up to speak after my reading, and the theme was consistent: Kevin's generosity in our world was unmatched. It was beautiful, wonderful, touching, sad yet wonderful to remember him, to realize what an impact he made on his family and friends. A life that touched so many others, one needlessly shortened.

Let us remember, let us move on. Can I? I can. Will I? In my mind I thought, well, you've moved from minute to minute, upon first hearing of his death, to hour to hour to get to this day, to get through that poem. Logically the next step is day to day, month to month . . . I can and I will.

Precursor #1

We all have different beliefs about what happens to a person when they leave us; I hadn't given it a whole lot of thought before Kevin died, even though I'd experienced the death of my mother some 13 years before and felt like she'd "visited" me after her passing. So, in a way I suspected that while a person is taken from us physically, the spirit continues to be with us. I hadn't thought about Kevin being with me after his death until he made himself known; then of course I wanted him to come more often, perhaps to validate that what had happened the first time wasn't some fluke. What happened is this: a friend had visited and reminded me that with just two days before the wake that I should contact some of Kevin's friends who were not my friends—looking though his address book, etc. Of course he was right, and he offered to make a few calls for me while I decided to turn on Kevin's computer and figure out whom else to tell by browsing his on-line contacts.

I carried my cell phone up to the office with me and set it aside, just in case someone needed to reach me. As I began to draft the letter I'd send to his friends, tears just welled up and I became so deeply sad. Six inches from the keyboard where my fingers were poised, the picture on my cell phone—of my cat, Mirepoix—suddenly changed, I kid you not. I gasped out loud; the picture before my eyes was of Betty Park, a nearby place that Kevin and I had been to, and he knew I went to, for solace. It was small, tiny in fact, but it had a body of water, and water has always been my serenity, my medium for strength and calm. I don't know how to explain that, being a Sagittarian, a "fire" sign, but I know I love the ocean and could never live far from it. So here is presented to me, as I struggle with this message, this photo of Betty Park, with its mirror-like lake in the background, delivered by some unknown force trying to tell me that it's OK, to be calm and find strength and that I'll get through it. How could I possibly think it was anyone but Kevin looking over my shoulder, understanding my pain, and wanting to help me? His love and generosity crossed over, and I was excited. I was ecstatic! I sent an IM to my sister Robyn and told her that this wonderful "thing" had happened. I did pick up the phone to look at the photo more closely, to make sure I wasn't just seeing things, and I even opened the phone and simply stared at the picture. When I closed it the phone, the picture should have reverted to my set background of Mirepoix the cat, but instead it remained Betty Park, but only for a little while—I watched it slowly fade to grey. And I thanked Kevin and finished the letter I'd drafted to his friends, many of whom I'd never met. I wasn't surprised when some of them were present at his service.

Precursor #2

I have never, ever, felt such deep physical pain to parallel my emotional sorrow when the realization hit me that Kevin was dead. Of course I asked the question "what do you mean he's dead?" as though the messenger (Kevin's stepfather) was somehow being cagey or lying. The message was quite clearly stated, but it wasn't quite clearly sinking in. Oh, when it did. How the deepest part of me just ached in a way I cannot even describe. I howled; I really did. And then the "practical" me realized that on this glorious August morning all the windows in the house were open and my neighbors likely thought there was something terribly wrong, only I wasn't about to tell them. I shut the windows and resumed my place on the floor screaming out and crying with emotion I'd never ever experienced, and hope to never again.

Not Quite 48

I buried Kevin with his prized Derrick Thomas #58 jersey, as he once or twice told me he wanted, on August 16. Somewhere shortly after that it came across my eyes that my first marriage, which ended in divorce, ended on exactly that date some 12 years before. August, from this point forward, will not be a month easily forgotten and one perhaps a bit dreaded. Some four weeks later would have been Kevin's 48th birthday. I wasn't quite sure what to do about it—Kevin never thought much of his birthday (or anyone's for that matter, though he always did something small and special when mine rolled around in December). I knew his sister Lee Ann was struggling mightily with his death and from the moment she woke up that day she'd have no other thought but of him. I drove to her home where she thoughtfully presented me with a birthday present—a lovely wooden statue of two women, one standing behind the other, hugging. The gift said it all. One of Kevin's friends sent me a text message that it was the first of many milestones that I'd face, and it was implicit that I'd conquer them all. I'm still day to day at this point in my life without Kevin, and while sadness overwhelms me, the day closes and I am another day behind me.

The Connection

The last words I said to Kevin were "I love you" and "I hope you feel better." He didn't respond, but I wasn't surprised—we were at odds with how he was taking care of himself, or not as the case may be, and while I know, *I know* he loved me beyond measure, he didn't say I love you back. I don't regret that, nor does he I suspect; it didn't really need to be said. Yet, still, I wasn't with him when he died—nobody was—and I had this desire to connect in some way and "hear" something from him. I wanted to know if he'd been in pain, if he'd been cognizant of what was happening at that moment when he gave up his physical being.

My dear friend Barbara reminded me at dinner one night shortly after that she had an acquaintance who was a medium, and that perhaps when the time felt right I should talk with him, perhaps make that connection I was thinking about. My first thought was that I wouldn't do it, but the idea stayed with me long enough for me to begin to think, each time that I was at home longing for Kevin, that perhaps I would—if only to be able to be with him once more.

There are far too many details around the actual appointment with the medium to scribe; the highlights are enough to make anyone start thinking about the abilities of a select group of individuals to help the rest of us talk with those who have crossed over. Here's a few: during my second phone call with the medium, to reschedule the original appointment, he'd asked me who "Kathryn" was. When I recovered, I told him it was Kevin's mother, whom Kevin was extremely close to and whom he'd missed dearly when she passed away some 13 years before him. To me, Kathryn is not a common name; for the medium to have suggested that she was there, well, it got my attention. There were other comments during our time together that also made me believe that the medium was indeed a communicator between the known and the "spirit" world—while he knew nothing about me, he saw that I was "surrounded by books" (I'm an avid reader and I work for a publishing company); he told me Kevin said he liked my hair—Kevin loved my hair, and loved to touch it; he told me that when Kevin is in the house with me he sits in the white chair in the back room—indeed, I have a white leather chair in the back of the house, in the room where I would spend a lot of time reading and Kevin would come and sit with me.

You get the picture—while I will admit that while I was there I was tentative and even a little disappointed that the revelations weren't all on the mark and more specific, in hindsight I can say it was very revelatory for me. I learned an immense amount from the medium about what happens to our souls when we cross over, and the true meaning of karma. Most important of all, though, was that I realized an utter sense of serenity after that meeting. I understood why Kevin died, how he died, and how much he truly, truly loved me. When Kevin told me through the medium to move on, that it was okay, there was something both liberating and final about Kevin's death–perhaps my "closure." The few times in life that Kevin and I had conversations about death—who would go first (always him, and before 50), who would manage better—Kevin would say that he would be devastated if I died first. I think a part of me felt like I needed to carry on his legacy of mourning the loss for the rest of my existence. But after those words "move on" were spoken, I'd felt like I'd received my release from a curse of never-ending sorrow. Five months later, moving on is a work in progress.

Engraved in Stone

Choosing the stone to mark Kevin's grave was relatively easy, albeit a very sad task. I found it oddly coincidental that as we (Kevin's sister and stepfather) entered the monument's showroom that the song "I Will Remember You" was playing in the background—I'd thought to play that during Kevin's service because we both loved the song and also because it was played during the service the Chiefs' had on their opening day after Derrick Thomas, Kevin's favorite football player, passed away. It made me feel like Kevin was with us in the room as we filed passed the various shapes, colors and finishes of granite before us.

The marker would be placed, hopefully, before Thanksgiving. My first thought was that it would come as no surprise to me if I got the call on our wedding anniversary, always right around that day, that the stone was installed. It didn't quite happen like that—the evening before I went to see the medium I was unusually restless; I just couldn't get comfortable and slept poorly. I also woke with stomach distress that kept me from being able to leave the house for a while. I finally decided to simply wait for the mail before starting my errands, and lo and behold in the mailbox was the card from the monument office stating that the stone had been placed. I first called Kevin's sister, Lee Ann, since she may not have known—I thought perhaps she'd seen it, though I suspect she'd have called me if she did. I told her about how I was trying to get out the door but my stomach wasn't letting me, and she too had the same problem that morning. We both decided we'd get to the cemetery that day; I left within a few minutes, figuring my stomach had settled enough and if not I could deal with it.

What I hadn't anticipated was dealing with seeing Kevin's name engraved in stone for the first time. It was like being punched very hard in the stomach so that all the air escapes your body and you have this deep, deep hollow pain in your abdomen. I cried so hard the pain became worse. I bent down to touch the letters, almost as though to see if it were real. It reminded me of the hours after Kevin's death when I was alone, and while I'd spoken to his stepfather on the phone, I had not seen anyone—perhaps it was a dream? I kept pinching myself that day until Kevin's eldest sister crossed the threshold of my front door and hugged me, and I said to her softly, *now I know it's real.* It was the same thing here—the finality of Kevin's death hitting me again, somehow harder this time. The sheer weight of it startled me—while I hadn't expected it would be easy to witness the marker, I never thought I'd react so strongly.

Coming slightly back to my senses at the gravesite I realized that it had started raining and that I could barely stand, and before I found myself on the ground I walked the ten feet or so back to the car and just stared at the name and just cried. I took out my camera phone and snapped a shot. I texted a note to my sister Robyn, my pillar of strength so many times in the last few months, and she sent me a warm hug from across the wire. I sent a note to Kevin's good friend J, the person Kevin told me he trusted the most of his cadre of friends. I stayed a long while, and then suddenly has this notion that I had to do something to make Kevin feel more comfortable in that space—I had to find something to put at his gravesite, and not flowers or a grave blanket, which were not Kevin's thing, but something that would make him laugh and smile (and make me do the same).

Heading out of the cemetery, I saw Lee Ann's car coming toward me and we pulled up side by side. I had to laugh a little when she asked me if I was okay to drive—I knew I must have looked like hell, but I was on a mission, and the cemetery is barely five miles from home. We talked a bit, shared some recent moments of feeling Kevin with us, and I headed off.

Finding something at home was harder than I thought—one of the very first tasks I took on when Kevin died was to clean his office, which was filled with boxes and envelopes full of papers along with shelves of dusty plastic action figures and toys he'd collected over the years. When Kevin was alive I'd often chide him to clean up the place—the dust was so thick you couldn't tell what the true color of anything in the room was—and he made a half-hearted effort to keep me at bay. As I was cleaning I found myself talking to him, laughing out loud about how he must have known that it would be the first room I'd attack. I did find what I was looking for—two plastic Kansas City Chiefs' helmets and a roll of clear packing tape. On my way out I spotted a single white faux rosebud I had in a vase near the door; I instinctively picked that up as well. Back to the cemetery I went to tape the helmets at the base. Kevin's sister had placed some faux fall flowers and a gourd there as well. I taped the rose to the stone, and am repeatedly surprised each time I return to the site at how they've managed to stay stuck through rain, sleet, snow, and gusts of wind.

The Anniversary that Wasn't

Kevin and I were married in Negril, Jamaica; each year following we celebrated our anniversary at the same resort, with the exception of the year before Kevin's death—we simply couldn't afford it. On our wedding anniversary the year he died, I didn't give much thought to what to do. It fell on the day after Thanksgiving, a day I would traditionally have off from work. For a milestone, it was strangely uneventful—I took the time to think about how wonderful our wedding was, and recalled each consecutive year that we returned to Swept Away to celebrate with friends we'd made there. I looked at the photo I have displayed of our five-year anniversary, where one of Kevin's dearest friends arranged for us to have dinner on the beach, surrounded by tiki lights and soft music competing with the sound of the ocean behind us. It was a beautiful night in every way imaginable, and we both look very happy in the picture—I know we were. This year the milestone was, except for those moments, just another day, and not even terribly sad—sad yes, but softened with a tinge of having wonderful memories to look back to. Perhaps I was reaching that turning point where, instead of every reminder of Kevin bringing me to tears of sadness, I was focusing on the "good stuff" and, having accepted his death, found some way of smiling first.

I was moving on—from one minute at a time during the first hours of Kevin's death, to one day at a time to get through the service, the myriad of calls to handle the legal/financial necessities, to one week at a time as each milestone crept closer and then, gratefully, the milestone was behind me.

An Uneventful 47

Kevin wasn't much for birthdays—certainly not his, which he termed just another day. He always remembered mine; always acknowledged it in some way, whether it be a nice dinner out or a nice dinner in, depending on our finances. This year it fell on a Saturday—one where the weather several days before had been predicted to be inclement. At first I thought I'd spend time with my family in northern New Jersey, and in fact had planned to visit a museum where a friend was displaying some of her art. When I thought more about it, the idea of driving 100 miles in potentially ugly weather became more unappealing, so I decided to have a nice dinner with Robyn on our usual Thursday night (that had been a tradition for years), and face my 47th birthday at home, on my own.

Naturally the weather forecast changed and the predicted bad weather wasn't arriving until the next day, but I was already resigned to making myself a nice dinner, buying a more expensive bottle of something than the usual $8.99 stuff (albeit always quite drinkable), and settling in with a good book or maybe a good movie, depending on what was up next on my Netflix queue. At the end of the day, it was just fine—I'd gotten a few calls, a few text messages from friends and family, and Mirepoix followed me everywhere and snuggled up to me all night. Hardly a suitable replacement for what would have been if Kevin were physically here, though I sense he inhabited the cat's warm body and chose to spend the night.

A Year without Santa Claus

Several years ago we'd decided to stop exchanging gifts—the first few years were a display of excessiveness that while fun, was a bit over the top. When Kevin was working, which was for all but the last two years of his life, we treated each other marvelously well all year long—numerous trips, nice dinners, little luxuries—all that made trying to celebrate Christmas with gifts almost silly. Our later approach was to settle in front of a fire with a good bottle of bubbly after having spent the Eve with Kevin's family, and simply toast another wonderful year together. So, on the first Christmas Eve of Kevin's passing I didn't miss wrapped gifts under the tree (we rarely put a tree up in recent years anyway); I simply missed Kevin. In fact, there was a bottle of champagne, a 2000 Tattinger La Reve blanc de blancs, idling on the wine rack we kept in the basement. It probably comes as no surprise that, post Christmas, it still remained there.

I did go to see Kevin's family on Christmas Eve—it had been how I'd spent the last 12 eves—and I knew that there'd be some tears shed. In fact, on my drive over they were already flowing. I have to pass the cemetery where Kevin is buried to get to his sister Lee Ann's house; I was compelled to pull in and stop for a few minutes. I'm not quite sure why; I can summon Kevin's spirit any time, anywhere, and there's no magic to seeing the headstone with his name expertly emblazoned across the heart-shaped marker. I just felt like he'd appreciate the gesture, and I will admit that having been there enough times already the shock of the first time is gone.

Lee Ann misses Kevin terribly; with each milestone she has her own memories, of course, many of which I have witnessed—and the Christmas Eve "tradition" was having Kevin make fun of her absurdly large meatballs. Lo and behold, as I was preparing my own plate, I noticed how they'd downsized this year, and even remarked that to her. We all manage our grief differently—some part of Lee Ann simply couldn't make them large enough to be made fun of if the person making fun of them wasn't around anymore.

I went home afterwards, poured a glass of wine, and put on some cello music to sit to with the cat. I sat near the white chair, lit the candles on the mantel that holds the photo of Kevin I'd happened across when searching for pictures of him to display at the service, and thought of past Christmases in that same space. No fire this year, no champagne this time, and, just perhaps, Kevin's spirit alongside me. But oh how I craved the *other* Kevin, the physical being who would have stroked my hair and told me I was his angel.

Naked Hands

Four and a half months after Kevin died I purposely walked out of the house without my engagement and wedding rings on—a milestone after almost ten years. It felt odd. I'd always been one to feel for it, probably because it was an expensive, beautiful engagement ring that I never wanted to leave behind no matter where I was. I've been ambivalent about the wear-it-or-not issue: leaving it behind was supposed to be a step toward moving on, and I was no longer married, so why pretend? On the other hand, I wasn't quite ready to *not* be married, which I guess means I didn't want there to be anyone looking and thinking I was "available." Of course I was just going to the local supermarket, not some place where I'd expected to be showcased as a single "available" woman. It was an uneventful trip and I came home and put them both on, along with Kevin's ring, which I'd become accustomed to wearing on the same finger as my own rings since he'd died—before that I was wearing his ring on my right hand because Kevin had gained weight over the years and could no longer slide it on his own ring finger. The day of his service, my fingers thinned a bit from the stress and not having eaten well several days prior, I wore it on a simple gold chain around my neck.

I tried again to leave the rings behind when heading to the office one day; getting ready to exit the house, it just didn't feel right. OK, so I wasn't ready to tell the world I was no longer a married woman. That milestone will have to wait a bit longer.

Welcome the New Year

Except for the previous year, again due to financial constraints, Kevin and I would spend our New Year's Eve in Philadelphia, mostly at the Ritz Carlton and often with good friends. Neither of us cared much for resolutions, and even though relatively young we didn't always see midnight. Tasked with the question from family and friends about how I would spend this one, the first after Kevin's death, I mostly shrugged and said no big deal, I'll be home. My dear friend Barbara offered to have me join her and her niece in DC for the night, and while the offer was gracious, it was not tempting—I knew I'd be okay being home, and while it may have been more fun to be there, a part of me just didn't want to be that far from home. And for no good reason; I just felt like since I'd be fine ringing in this New Year at my own place that it didn't feel compelling to do anything else.

It started feeling like a long day, with the time moving slowly, which would mean perhaps a long night to get to the magical hour. I was reading a novel and alternately trying to polish off the Sunday Times crossword puzzle, and made some dinner. The novel hooked me and before long it was 11 pm—my first thought was, well, I can make it until midnight at this stage. I decided to bang on the computer in the office a bit, draft my Happy New Year message to send seconds before to my family via text messaging, and before I knew it yet another milestone had passed. In truth, they were getting easier. I knew they would, I just hadn't figured it would happen this quickly.

Travelocity, Expedia, or Orbitz?

I'd decided a week before the holidays that I was tired—yes, physically, but more than that; it was also a feeling of carrying a weight, of not ever quite feeling warm enough, and of just needing to be someplace else. I'd taken a lot of time off around the holidays to use up accrued vacation that couldn't carry over, but it wasn't truly relaxing. Being in the house I'd shared with Kevin for the last nine years, I was now always looking at it as a project—shred this pile of old papers, sort and pack this closet for Goodwill, decide what can be tossed in Monday night's trash. The answer I had in mind was a quick getaway to someplace close, where I could be there in just a few hours and be on a beach within an hour of arrival. Based on the east coast, there are many options, but I wanted to go by the end of January and there aren't that many places in the states that are warm enough—I thought Vieques, mostly because a good friend had told me how beautiful it was, but that meant a short flight from Puerto Rico, and that was too much effort. I hadn't been to Florida since I was 16—that was a trip to Kissimmee with my sister Robyn, mostly to sit by the pool and see what Disney had to offer in 1976, which by the way wasn't much—Epcot wasn't even there yet. I'd never been to Miami, and so that was where I focused my search. But oh, how to start?

For all of our time together—that would be eleven and a half years—Kevin was the travel agent of our relationship. And my gosh, he was so good at it; he enjoyed it, and always did a fabulous job with making the arrangements, sweet-talking the right people into various and sundry upgrades, luxuries, etc., and never failing to make a trip memorable in some way or another. He was the brains and energy behind our Negril wedding, complete with 30+ guests who joined us there, making just about all of their arrangements as well. So, staring in front of a computer screen to make my own travel arrangements, I wasn't even sure frankly where to begin. I'd narrowed down the where, but the how was less obvious—do

I start with one of those package deals from the well-known places, or do I book separately through the airline and hotel? I was smart enough to figure out that I'd have to spend a few hours researching both avenues and then seeing what the best deal was. And I did that, for hours. In the back of my mind I knew that I was actually procrastinating from committing to the vacation—on more than one occasion I'd found a place that was within the range of what I wanted to spend, but each time I was hesitant—maybe if I wait one more day? Some of the hesitancy came from wanting to stay at a place what was full service—I wasn't quite sure I'd be ready to take on the streets of Miami to fend for dinner, so staying at a hotel that had a decent restaurant or more than one that I could stick with during my stay sounded comforting. I kept bouncing back to Trip Advisor to see what previous guests had to say about the lodging, the food, and the location— trying to keep in mind that you can't please everyone, of course.

After two days of intermittently searching, deciding, then saying I'll do it tomorrow, I had to laugh at myself and just say "do it"—it's four days, you're not that particular about where you stay as long as it's clean and the ocean is just steps away, and everything will fall into place no matter what you choose. SoBe it.

With This Ring

Our minister in Jamaica made a beautiful speech about the eternity of love, comparing its symbol, the ring, as round, never ending. Kevin often recalled that speech, and that minister, even though he was not religious. Kevin believed in the sentiment more than he believed in the physical act of wearing the ring—while he indulged me, he didn't see the wearing of his wedding ring as the manifestation of that love. Nor did I, in fact; when he gained a few pounds and the ring no longer fit him comfortably I took to wearing it for him, on my right hand. It made me smile when I glanced at it.

On the day of his service, I wore it on a simple gold chain around my neck—it was too big to fit on any of my fingers. Then I took to wearing his ring on my left hand, slipping it on first before my own wedding band and engagement ring. Daily. There was some small sense of taking something of Kevin with me each day before I left the house. I didn't care that I was a widow nor did I really care what others thought.

I began to think about not wearing any rings a few days after I began to train a new hire at my company. You invariably start talking about your personal life, and I got a little spooked about him asking me about my husband, and felt like I'd make the situation awkward by having to explain that he was dead but I was still showing off three rings. Was it time to go bare?

On the weekend after that person started, I opened the box that Kevin first gave me the engagement ring in. My 37th birthday. The Four Seasons, Santa Barbara. A lovely four-inch by three-inch box, adorned with angels. Of course, inside, a jewelry box. Honestly, my first thought was a pair of earrings. On that night, when I opened the box, I gasped; mostly in surprise, somewhat in delight. I closed the box immediately, positively stunned at its contents. Kevin reopened the box and asked me to marry him. I asked him if he was sure;

frankly, we'd had a bit of a tumultuous courtship, which is why I hadn't expected him to ask me to marry him. He told me that he thought of his life with me, then without me, and knew that there was no choice but the former. I accepted—albeit a few hours later when he reminded me that I'd never actually said "yes"!

I reopened that larger box ten years and just about three weeks later. Inside were the rose petals I'd gathered from those adorning the bed in our suite. A champagne cork—a 1990 Dom Perignon—was resting among the dried petals. I slowly, very deliberately placed all three rings in the velvet slit from the original engagement ring box, recalling wonderful memories of that night.

And so my hand is bare, but oh how my heart is full.

(My) Life After Death

Kevin's Big Love

Sports has been a big part of my life even before Kevin entered it—I was a huge baseball fan (to wit: my high school graduation caption says "Future Mrs. Bucky Dent"). I went to a high school where basketball was all that, and attended as many games as I could as a cheerleader in the stands. I fell in love with Michael Jordan while he did Food Lion commercials while he was at UNC; I was dating my first husband, whose grandparents lived in Norfolk where the commercials aired regularly.

Kevin grew up on the ice—he played hockey from the time he could hold the stick through his final year at Drexel University some twenty years later. He tried out for the Olympic team, but at barely five-foot six inches he wasn't quite what they had in mind. He was lightning quick and knew where to hit you. Better than that, he knew where to get the puck in the net, and did often. He could barely stand watching professional hockey—he was exasperated by the inefficiency of many a players' inability to find the spot that was oh so obvious to his skilled eye. I might add that he was the sexiest thing on skates; I simply loved watching him, and was awed by his ease; I had learned to skate as a teenager and was so tentative, often afraid of falling hard; for Kevin it was as natural as walking. I think I envied him that.

He took my love of basketball quite seriously during our courtship—I saw both of Jordan's retirement games, in Chicago and then Philly. We became season ticket holders for the Philadelphia 76ers. Allen Iverson had just come into the league; the team was rebuilding, and while they lost well more than they won, Iverson was worth watching. Kevin, a bit of an introvert, became the favorite of everyone in our section—the beer guys whom he regularly over-tipped; the ushers, with Kevin always giving a kind word and conversation about their families and the "how ya doin'" mentality of South Philly. And the media too—he always stopped to chat with local "celebs." One thing about Kevin: he always made you feel important, and he truly, genuinely, cared about you.

Within a few days of his passing I contacted our ticket representative, and a few weeks later she asked me if I'd like to bring some family and friends to a game, gratis—maybe a luxury suite or two, with all the trimmings? The gesture floored me—this is an NBA team, not your local high school or college organization; again Kevin's impact becomes strikingly apparent. A few months after the initial conversation 34 of his friends sat in two luxury suites and enjoyed a wonderful night of memories. I kid you not: as I traveled from conversation to conversation that night, someone was telling a Kevin story. Gosh how it warmed me, and made me realize how much others truly cherished knowing him. That night the Sixers presented me with a framed jersey, aptly emblazoned with Kevin's last name and the number "1", which sits less than four feet away from me now. What a remarkably apt symbol of his years of loyalty to the game and to all of those involved in the game. It made me recall, too, the beautiful lilies the 76ers had sent over to Kevin's service, with a short, simple note about how he would be missed.

So what was I to do with 41 home games we'd already signed up for? I channeled Kevin and donated several to charity, freely gave several tickets away to family and friends, sold some to the usual suspects who'd always bought from us because are seats are pretty fabulous, and then kept a few for me to attend. The first game where I sat in our seats happened as a continuation of a long-standing tradition—Kevin had always taken my nephew to a game for his birthday, and my heart told me it was right to keep that annual rite intact. I sat in Kevin's seat; the ushers in our section hugged me hard and long; the beer guy sought me out to extend his condolences. And hey, the Sixers won. My nephew RJ and I reminisced about what it was like to have Kevin at the game, and how much we missed him. I recall no less than four times of having to breathe deeply and not cry.

And I did not. Instead RJ and I roared and hooted and, in those final seconds, I realized I'd conquered one more milestone.

London Calling

Several weeks after Kevin's death my director sent an e-mail aptly titled "London calling." Our sister organization in the United Kingdom was seeking an experienced trainer to cross the pond, and I'd be a prime candidate having worked with them over the last few years. In a split second my mind registered "wow" and I'd asked Matt to find out if my salary in dollars would travel with me in pounds to Britain, and he said he'd ask.

Upon further reflection, truly just hours later, I realized that barely two months after Kevin's death that I could not consider the offer; I was still raw from his passing and I needed the support I was getting daily from friends, colleagues, and family. While there was a bit of excitement about the prospect, deep in my heart I knew it was not the right time, and I had to let the opportunity pass. I'd sent a message to Matt telling him that, but he was in transit between Manila and Mumbai and wouldn't see it before the next work day, and here it was Friday. The UK manager called me on Monday before Matt could tell him that my interest was, at least for now, fleeting, and I had to explain that given my personal situation it was not the right time for the opportunity, and if it had been six months down the road . . .

Fast forward to five months later, and an e-mail from the same manager: was the timing better? Think, Donna. What is there to keep you here? Yes, family. But how often do you see them? Well, Robyn once a week for dinner. And yet, she and the rest will always be there, a phone call, a text or instant message away. Yes, friends; but don't you have some contacts in the UK, and don't you make friends somewhat easily? Yes, colleagues at the same company for the past 25 years. But won't they still be there? And haven't you already made good contacts with some of the UK staff?

We all have our comfort zones. Hey, I have a beautiful home, and I love where I live. What's the down side to taking the plunge and the job? While I do have that lovely home, it's far too much house for me and the cat. It's really not that close to where many of my friends are—they are 100 miles north, where my job is and where I grew up. While it's close to Cape May, my vortex that restores my sanity, my energy, then again, does the body of water matter, or just being close enough to one?

I ask for my salary requirements. And I wait for a response. My biggest concern: how will my 18-year-old cat Mirepoix deal with separation anxiety?

Photo Op

Kevin was a talented, amazing photographer—our home has always been a showcase to his talent: just about every room has a framed picture of his, and whenever we had guests they would always remark at what an eye Kevin had. When he was in his teens he followed bands like Heart and Yes and Genesis and took photographs, got backstage passes, lived a little bit of the "Almost Famous" life. (In a rather strange turn of events, Cameron Crowe, director of that film, wound up marrying Kevin's wannabe flame, Nancy Wilson.)

I'd always been one to keep a camera with me when vacationing, but my eye was nowhere as keen as Kevin's. On my first vacation without him at my side, to Miami, I snapped a whopping 16 photos. Kevin would have taken 316, and nearly all of them would have been frame-worthy. It wasn't that I didn't see dozens more photo opportunities—Miami's beaches are beautiful, and the neon of Collins Avenue, the views from Ocean Drive and the bustle of Lincoln Road are prime fodder. Even with camera in hand, I often bypassed shots with the lingering thought that Kevin would have simply clicked; I don't know if it was that I couldn't compete with his photos or if I just wanted to leave that part be—in other words, to see the shot in my mind's eye, but to forgo it knowing that photographing those moments meant far less without Kevin to frame the moment as well as the photo.

The trip to Miami was sorely needed R&R, though I'll admit to my moments of missing Kevin deeply, knowing how much he'd have loved to be there—he lived for the next vacation. Reggae music coming from the hotel next door had me in tears at the pool one afternoon. Still, I'd managed to pass another milestone in planning and taking a vacation without him. I had friends tell me how proud they were of me; it was perhaps one of the easier accomplishments given it was almost entirely pleasurable, but I understood there was a little bit of triumph in it, too.

Beyond the Bridge

The first trip Kevin and I ever took together was to San Francisco, then on to Napa and wine country. I had been back to SF on business very shortly after Kevin's death—it was my re-introduction to the work force for a very focused project that I felt would be good for me. I did spend some time with friends in the city, though I told friends in Yountville that I just wasn't ready to cross the bridge. Kevin loved wine and wine country—his "dream" job was to be a cellar rat or a pour person at a winery (to which one of his dearest friends, a winemaker, said was a "pussy" job). We'd looked into it once—an opportunity that came up for me to transfer to the SF office—but the opportunity never panned out.

My second business trip in less than seven months brought me back to SF, and this time I decided I would rent a car and travel with a friend into Novato for dinner with a couple we both knew, then on to Napa the next day to visit friends, maybe taste, just drive around and take in the beauty of the vineyards. I liked the idea of having company—it would keep me at least slightly preoccupied and give me a chance to talk out how I was feeling. But it wasn't meant to be—my friend's father needed surgery in Miami so I was on my own.

The hardest stop I couldn't make: Domaine Carneros. If you've never been it's breathtaking: a chateau on a hill with gorgeous views of the surrounding terraced landscape of vine after vine. It was a favorite, and usually the first stop, as Kevin and I headed into wine country. There are umbrellaed tables outside where staff brings you samples of mostly bubbles, though they offer some still wines, and tasty little crackers with a spread of some sort. You can order a cheese plate, or caviar, and take in the whole wonderful, complete experience with your wine. Someday I do want to climb those stairs up to the patio and order something sparkling, but I had barely been able to breathe when I drove past it; I wasn't ready this outing.

I did manage some other of our "usual" things to do—I picked up lunch at the Oakville Grocery, found a nice spot to park, opened the sun roof and found the "real" jazz station on XM radio and enjoyed the moments. I drove to St. Helena—there's one spot on Main Street where the trees on either side of the road are tall and almost form an arch—it's incredibly beautiful when the trees are in full bloom, and this being very early March they were not, but the scene was lovely just the same (and I even snapped a photo, since the traffic along Main was at a veritable crawl).

I miss Kevin terribly in so many moments across the bridge; and yet, at the same time, it's not that aching sadness it used to be—the kind that physically hurt. It's more a melancholy that in short time turns to a snapshot of fond memory of all those wonderful times we had there. I will never *not* miss him, but I'm more certain now that I will smile more than cry when I revisit those moments of our lives we had in places near and far from home.

Shreds of the Past

Kevin was primarily self employed as a consultant for most of the time I knew him—he had a business, Rain Technology Group, Inc. (a spin on his last name which many people often pronounced incorrectly), and over the years he had employed friends. In his office a closet held three milk crates of business papers, and I knew that I couldn't simply put them out to trash without separating that which would be anonymous versus those papers that contained personal information such as social security numbers. It was the last closet to tackle—partly because it was the "pre-Donna" years; two dozen photo albums of the life Kevin had before I entered in 1996.

I hadn't expected to find anything worth keeping in that closet—yes, a few photo albums to give to friends: Kevin's trip to Japan with his best man, Dan; the trips he took with J to Jamaica; childhood photographs to pass along to his sister, Lee Ann. I started one very rainy, cold Saturday morning after breakfast and the piles grew quickly. I was attentive to shred anything that had personal information, even Kevin's; while his Social Security and Taxpayer ID numbers would certainly be red flags if someone tried using them, I felt better feeding the shredder. I worked backwards—I saw folders marked 1986!

The "find" came in 1996. It was the year Kevin and I met, and while sorting through the toss or shred I came upon the Year-end Summary from American Express. I knew Kevin would always use his card—he collected miles at any opportunity—and I realized I'd held in my hand the summary of our first year together; I was actually a little excited.

I only fleetingly glanced at the period before May 3—the day we met for lunch in Philadelphia—I saw a trip to the Bahamas in March, and wondered if that was with his ex, but didn't dwell on it.

Oh, what a year we had. Our first date in May: La Champignon-Tokio, Philadelphia: $214.20; I recall a bottle of Perrier Jouet rose, and my first taste of sushi. Later that month: The Huntington Hotel in San Francisco: $889.79; I lied to my mother and said I was staying with a friend. Fleur de Lys: $528.90. The Vintage Inn, Yountville: $610.21; the first time I'd stayed in wine country. Then, in July: Little Dix Bay, Virgin Gorda: $3,377.55; we had our own island for the day—George Dog—and I remember the day I told Kevin I loved him.

That was life with Kevin; frequent travel, wonderful food and wine . . . I had to put the summary aside. It became a bit difficult to look at through my tears, and I did want to keep it intact. Several days later I was able to pull it out of the desk drawer again and take another look—it was less sad, still wonderful. I am so happy to have had all that pleasure with Kevin. I don't care if I never have quite the same experience again; it was more than enough for a lifetime. I used to tell Kevin I was a "coach" girl at heart who could live far more simply than the first-class life he was able to show me for a good part of our time together. Kevin, however, was not meant for coach!

Saying Goodbye to Home

London returned the call; negotiations complete, I am now preparing to say goodbye to the home Kevin and I made together for ten years. Oh, how daunting, yet everything falls into place in a manner that is, truly, not of this world. I decide to take the opportunity to live and work in London for a year; I place my house for sale and it sells, in a recession-like market, in two weeks—and at a price I am happy with. I find a home for my cat. I find a thrift store that will take the aging exercise equipment, the old computer stuff, and the loveseat I'd had since 1987 from my first marriage. People come to help me pack, sort, and get through the emotions. My closing is less than a week away. I've packed just about all my photos, though the one of Kevin and me laughing out loud as we sit at the edge of a catamaran on its way to Rick's Café in Negril sits before me. I am at once so excited by the adventure before me, and yet so filled with anxiety each day and at night that I've taken to keeping Benadryl at my bedside, even though I hate the way it makes me feel in the morning.

I'm doing this; I'm really doing this . . . Jim, Kevin's stepfather, seems happy for me. I have not heard from Kevin's eldest sister since my announcement at Easter that I was jetting to London to interview for the job. Kevin's sister whom he was closest with is understandably having trouble with this—she told me on Easter that she sensed that all that is Kevin is slowly going away . . . and yet I feel differently about that. Kevin is with me every day; he has guided me through this entire affair of selling our home, sorting through I can't even begin to tell you how much "stuff" (two bedrooms, two offices, a living room, a family room, a dining room . . . I'm guessing over 150 wine glasses). He has kept me calm, I know.

I remember that when I went to see the medium, he told me that my guiding spirit's name was Helena. She and I talk often now; I feel I need strength to simply get through the day sometimes. I'm sore as all hell. My family and friends have been beyond generous with time and muscle to get through everything in this beautiful, wonderful home that I will miss deeply. I go through old cards Kevin and I sent each other; dozens of photos; room after room of memory. Oh how much romance, how much love, how much depth in these ten years we shared. How I miss him so when it all comes flooding back and I think how it's just not right, not fair, that he is not here with me now. I believe in karma; what in the world happened his last time out?

I sit out on the deck in the back at night with a glass of wine and recall how Kevin and I would do the same and watch the stars come out. I cry silently, of course—the ache of not having Kevin inches away still hurts, and still sometimes deeply—and yet I have come around to thinking that he is OK with all of this, and the relatively smoothness to which all of this has come together gives me faith that he is guiding my thoughts and helping me through an incredibly stressful time.

London calls, I answer. Summer in Europe? I am ready.

(My) Life After Death

Saying Hello . . . Cheerio

In what can only be described as a swift whirlwind of activity, I am in London. And I am happy. I am tired, which is a small price to pay for having managed to tidy up affairs in the states and arrive here (on a Tuesday morning with the first day at the office planned for Wednesday). One 61-pound suitcase, one laptop case and a backpack were all that traveled with me—enough to get me through two weeks. I anticipated that after that I'd have my sister ship a second (and less heavy) suitcase sitting in her apartment, which is where I idled between closing on the house on May 12 and arriving at Gatwick on May 27. Those were, blissfully, uneventful weeks—preparing to go; tidying up the US office details; trying to spend time with Robyn since she has been my best friend for ages and it was understandable we'd miss each other deeply when I left. Spending time with friends and other family who all promised to visit once I settled in London. There were some tears, but in hindsight the departure wasn't nearly as emotional as I'd thought—it was a sign to me that I was ready to move on.

So how does one go about settling in London? Well, the work transition was easy, more or less—I know the team, the work, the environment, but I don't know everything I need to train editors on and that will come in time. The flat rental was a bit more daunting—so many letting agents, so many areas to look at, and with London being as expensive as it is, so many decisions to make about how much is the right amount to spend and not be so far out of the city to enjoy it. I had contacted three letting agents and worked with two (the other never responded after my initial consultation). North, south, west and east all have postal codes that are within my budget, with some being more distant that others. I'd hoped to stay on the fringes of Zone 1 even if it was in Zone 2 (on the tube map) and had done some online searching before I flew; it seemed possible to stay within a half hour of the office.

The first few flats I saw were disappointing, to say the least—it was déjà vu to searching for a reasonably-priced apartment in Hoboken and having to step over mounds of other people's messes and try to ignore stained ceilings, small spaces and ugly bathrooms. For Hoboken it was love at first sight in a brownstone uptown that was bare of furnishings and relatively clean. I recall asking the property agent what I needed to secure the place before someone else did—like London, good apartments have a tendency to go quickly.

In London, it was more "really like" at first sight—a garden flat with two small bedrooms in North Kensington that was clean, tastefully half-furnished (the bedroom furniture was yet to be delivered) and reasonably light for a grey London afternoon and the flat being six steps down from the ground floor—big enough windows to let in light, but not the same as being on higher ground. It had its own entrance and a winding walkway to a garden that, while it was reserved (per the landlord's chap who did work on the building) for the renters in another apartment, I was certain I'd sweet-talk them into being able to use on occasion.

So why not just make an offer? Frankly I was still harboring hopes of living more centrally—I'd seen postings for flats in other areas in Central London that were in my price range, but was having trouble connecting with the agent. It felt like a hard decision; I kept trying to meditate, to channel Kevin, Helena, and whoever else was willing to help me make a decision. I cried. I panicked. I didn't sleep. I had a heart-to-heart conversation with the letting agent to help him understand why it was so difficult for me—yes, it was nice, especially for the price; yes, it was in a nice location—minutes from Portobello Road where there are shops, restaurants, and the market on the weekends. I think my hold-up was waiting for some "sign" that this was *the* place. I wanted to see more but there's such pressure here (whether real or imagined) to not let a good flat pass you by for another renter who would snap it up.

I had to laugh at myself for thinking it could be that easy and sure. In the end I put a deposit on the garden flat and decided I really did like the place, what I remember of it having seen so many flats in a short period. My dear friend Heike once told me that nothing is forever—if it turns out that I don't like it, I can decide that in four months, look for something else in the next two and leave after my "short let" six-month contract. I do think I will be happy there.

I spent the first London weekend taking the train to the underground stops nearby (two happen to be equidistant to the flat), looking at the neighborhood and getting a feel for where I'll buy food and hang out at a café on weekends. The second bedroom is a real luxury—with guests, a place for some privacy; without, a place to set up a home office and keep clothes, etc. I sat at a Pret for lunch and tried to do some budgeting—the flat rent is about a good chunk of my salary—more than what most experts would say you should spend—but I'm a single gal with little else to spend on, so I'll see how the first four months go and take it from there.

And, my first visitors have signed up—my sister Robyn for August. We've already decided that Paris is on the itinerary.

Gosh, life *is* good. Not without its sadness—I so often look at the photo I have of Kevin and while he is smiling and it feels so real, he is not here with me. He would love the adventure of London (though he always complained that he never wanted to move, and being the packrat that he was, it's clear why) and I would love to be having a glass of wine with him at some little outdoor café taking in the scene. He is always in my mind. As I take photos to post on my newly-started blog, I think of him and the beauty he saw and so easily captured with photographs—I could never measure up to his fantastic eye, but often as I see a scene I think, that would be a photograph Kevin would capture, and perfectly. Frame it.

Christmas in June

Making the flat my "home" meant getting my personal effects, 15 boxes at a friend's home in New Jersey, across the pond. I had decided not to purchase anything but essentials—towels to bathe, sheets to sleep, and yes, a spatula to turn eggs, always a nice Sunday morning treat for me. I was anxious to get my "stuff" and get it sorted out in the flat.

The funniest thing happened on the way to London for these boxes—attempting delivery twice while I was at work, I arranged delivery for a Monday evening after 5 pm. I was, quite honestly, disappointed; I wanted the boxes for the weekend so that I could get the articles settled and not have to worry about it during the work week. I had called the parcel delivery service too late on Friday to get them on the Saturday morning truck, and resigned myself to leaving work a little earlier than usual on Monday to be in the flat at five sharp and wait for the knock on the door.

On the Friday evening before a friend dropped by to see the flat, and we chatted for a bit. As we were getting ready to walk back to the tube, we spotted a gentleman who was looking for 46 "E" as in Edward; I inquired to the name and it was mine; he had misread the label "B" and would have never found "E"—there is none. Had Andros and I left a minute earlier we would have missed him; fortunately our timing was perfect and we unloaded the boxes from the truck into the bedroom. Andros smiled at me as I left him at the Latimer Road tube and said he knew that I'd be up all night now that my boxes were in the flat. He wasn't far from wrong—I returned to the flat at about 9:20 in the evening, and proceeded to slice open, unwrap, sort and place my goodies. By 1:30 in the morning I had everything unpacked, and for the most part in place. It felt wonderful to have my own belongings, and it made the flat mine.

I had moments of distress—some breakages of items that made me sad. The first was a small statuette I'd given Kevin some 12 years before of a Degas ballerina; the head had been broken off. I wrapped that piece myself, and clearly not quite well enough. I vowed to replace because it reminded me of Kevin and I wanted that token memory.

A box of china dishes that wasn't meant to come to London found its way—when I was packing up I had two sets of boxes, and this one clearly wound up on the wrong side of the basement. Half of the dishes were destroyed; I wound up, oddly enough, with a set of two of everything. Coincidence? I had to laugh out loud at Kevin's planning of an intimate dinner using the surviving dishes!

So as I scanned the room, I was happy—a half dozen photographs of Kevin's graced shelves or walls; I had some of my treasured books—Austen, Woolf; I have more CDs than I will probably listen to, but I was filling an 18 x 14 x 12 box and these were the CDs from Kevin's collection of over a thousand that I'd decided to keep. Lots of Beatles, Seal, and a nice holiday collection. A number of classical discs, a combination of Kevin's CDs and mine. The first that I listened to here: Bach cello suites. I recall when I was at my friend Heike's for dinner at her flat in NYC how she played some Bach, and it spoke to me. I went out and bought my own collection of cello suites (Gaspar Cassado, Pablo Casals) and listened to them quite often back home. There is something a bit haunting about them—no orchestra behind them, the single instrument almost moaning. I found them soothing then, and I still do.

And so life in London is settling in quite nicely, thank you. I feel like I belong. I've figured out the tube, the bus, the neighborhood in just two weeks. I like it here. I am snapping photos casually, posting them along with my adventures to a blog for friends and family to keep up with my life. And the time marches on—when 10 months since Kevin's death passed, on June 12, I paused. I still look at his photo daily, and I still talk to him. I do still feel his hand guiding my life here, but I must say, there is a part of me that feels it fading just a bit.

Is it that I'm adjusting, moving forward, moving on? I'm not sure. I do feel like it's been a lifetime since Kevin and I were physically in the same room. And it feels like I've been in London for far longer than the 30 days that I have been here. I think that's all good. I don't want to forget Kevin—I know I never will, in fact—and I feel like should I need him, he will know that, and he will be here. I mean, how is it that I arranged for those boxes to arrive on Monday after five and just as I am leaving the flat on a Friday evening the delivery person shows? I know what I know.

Time marches on, and still, thankfully, Kevin and I walk in step with each other. Gosh I do miss him, and yet I "get" that he has been here leading me in the direction of moving on, settling, and who knows what next. I suppose I shall see soon enough.

August in Paris

Kevin was meant to be with me in Paris; one Christmas he bought me Speak French in Your Car tapes so that I could practice—I told him I wanted to know some of the language, and that I wanted to get there before I turned 50.

Instead of Kevin I have my sister Robyn at my side, and I am standing in front of Notre Dame. I have been thinking of Kevin because the anniversary of his death is approaching, and because as I revisit the tourist stuff with Robyn I am reminded of Kevin's and my trip to London in 1997 and how wonderful it was—he was never without his camera, and many of the 16 x 20 prints that hung in our house were from London: Piccadilly Circus, a raven in the Tower; Big Ben; Trafalgar Square when pigeon feeding was still allowed. Some of those are with me in my London flat.

Approaching Notre Dame from across the Seine you are apt to be awestruck by its massive structure, its ornate beauty, and its dark energy. I take a few pictures, thinking how much fun Kevin would have had getting the gargoyles at the right angle for the perfect shot. I walk along the cathedral and I am struck with a deep sadness suddenly—I should be standing here with Kevin, and I am not. The afternoon tourists see me sobbing hard enough for my shoulders to shake. I am alone, and it is not fair, I am thinking—we were meant to be looking at this together. I don't know that I've felt that way before; while I've missed him, this feels like the first time I am almost distraught that he cannot be with me. Even in London I have often felt a deep ache that he is not here to enjoy this time with me, to take in this beautiful city with me.

Robyn consoles me and I am eventually calm; the moment has passed. I think I pretend that her shoulders are his, or perhaps they are his. We take in Coustou's Pieta from a distance; we are too late to enter for today. I find it interesting that many of the moments I've had of late have been at or near churches—in London just two weeks ago I found myself feeling the same sadness as I walked into St. Mary Abbots on one of my getting-to-know-London strolls. Kevin was not a religious person, nor am I; however, there is something of a spiritual awakening, if you will, that I feel when approaching the church that truly stirs my senses.

The rest of Paris is lovely, but my spirit is a bit less enthusiastic than earlier in the day.

First

There is nothing unusual about the day, except that I am back in the US for a fingerprint scan to obtain my entry visa to work in London for one year. I have no plans to visit the cemetery or to do anything in particular to mark the first anniversary of Kevin's death—I have dinner plans with family, and will go to the Newark office to catch up on some work mail. I will likely think of Kevin more often—in every moment of solitude—because of the date. No matter; I have become more comfortable with his loss; our conversations are funny more than sad. He has sent me comfort and I have finally embraced it. I am, truly, moving forward, moving on—and not without him, just without pain and with less sadness in my life, in my heart.

I thought that if my visa paperwork was expedited that I would borrow my sister's car and drive to the storage bin, perhaps pick up some additional photographs for my London flat and start putting serious thoughts around organizing a retrospective display of Kevin's photography. It wasn't meant to be and I stay for my week in the Newark/New York City area meeting with as many family and friends as I can; I don't expect to be back in the area any time soon. I call Kevin's family, too, since I will not see them. The day comes, the day goes. I fall asleep talking to Kevin about how I cannot believe it is a full year since he is gone. Sleep comes easily; I am perhaps a little disconcerted that the day was not marked by something more meaningful. But it is what it is.

And in the End

It is one year and one day after burying Kevin, and I am sitting on a plane flying back home—to London. I spent the previous week in the US to finalize my work permit and entry visa so that I can live and work in the UK until 2009. I am not sad. I am overwhelmed by my good fortune in the previous few months to have this opportunity.

The love you take is equal to the love you make . . . I have had that bit of a Beatles' lyric in my head for I don't know how long—probably as long as Kevin has been gone. In the end, Kevin made friends and cherished them like no other human being. He cared so much for people as if it were his sole desire; he felt he was put on this earth to help others, to make them happy in whatever way he could. Many times that was monetary—picking up the tab with old friends and new, or leaving an overly generous tip after chatting with the wait staff to learn some intimate detail. It wasn't always about money; Kevin found ways to be kind beyond money or measure. If he had what you needed, he'd give it to you; if he didn't, he'd find a way to help. I have literally seen him give the shirt off his back to people in Jamaica when we were vacationing there; he most certainly felt good about that, but it wasn't why he was doing it—there was simply something innate in Kevin that led him to give more and take less.

And, in the end, he has given me a love that will never diminish, far more than the love he took from me. I have found a wonderful place in my heart to celebrate our memories, and that makes me smile. I miss Kevin no less, yet I have become more comfortable with his physical being no longer being at my side because that has been replaced with a warmth that is as close to him lying next to me that I can hope for.

I will always carry him in my heart.

www.ingramcontent.com/pod-product-compliance
Lightning Source LLC
LaVergne TN
LVHW041500070426
835507LV00009B/723